Content Transformation
An Introduction to Enterprise Content Ops and Content Strategy

Celebrating 25 years

Content Transformation: An Introduction to Enterprise Content Ops and Content Strategy

For information, contact:
Scriptorium Publishing Services, Inc.
P.O. Box 12761
Research Triangle Park, NC 27709-2761
USA

info@scriptorium.com
scriptorium.com

Contents

What people are saying

"In my work to connect the academic and practitioner sides of technical communication, no other resource has been as useful as the online and print publications from Scriptorium. From *Technical Writing 101* to the Content Ops Manifesto, my teaching and research projects have frequently cited O'Keefe et al. I am looking forward to the next 25 years of publications about content and tweets about chocolate from the Scriptorium team."

—Carlos Evia, Professor and Associate Dean, Virginia Tech

"I was chatting with fellow Content Strategists about the biggest challenges they faced in rolling out projects. Not one person mentioned technology. Getting stakeholder buy-in, overcoming resistance to change—organizational friction points to overcome, as you mention in Scriptorium's Content Ops Manifesto."

—Jack Molisani, Executive Director, The LavaCon Conference

"In today's 'Experience Economy,' content experiences at every single touch point of the customer journey, from pre-purchase research to post-sale support, are both an opportunity for and a threat to brands. Today's customers demand that content experiences are rich and engaging, personalized and relevant, seamless and omnichannel, memorable and rewarding. This puts the people and processes, tools and systems, strategies and tactics around creation, management and delivery of content under spotlight. Scriptorium is one of the few consultancies uniquely positioned to address all these challenges around content strategy, by breaking down artificial silos across the enterprise."

—Saibal Bhattacharjee, Director of Product Marketing & Business Strategy, PPBU, Adobe Inc.

"Introducing a CCMS is not a content strategy. You need to define your content model first. Content is an essential part of your product. It helps you selling your products and keeping your customers happy. That is why you need to treat it with the same respect as the other parts of the product, like the code, for example."

—Ulrike Parson, CEO, parson AG

"The strategic approach to content and content systems is one of the fastest moving spaces in business today. The companies that are well organized and forward thinking are positioning themselves to capitalize on massive shifts in buyer behavior and customer experience. Scriptorium has has been at the forefront of this industry for decades, their work is more relevant and needed today than ever before."

—Patrick Bosek, CEO, Heretto

"When I was in a junior writer in the 1980s, few of us could even imagine the complexity of a content ecosystem and the capabilities on which we would all come to depend. It's not just writing: it's the business of content and the know-how that allows us to plan and execute intelligently. This collection demonstrates that Scriptorium continues to work at the forefront of content industry practitioners as consultants and thought leaders."

—Paul Perrotta, Content Organization Consultant

"Customers and employees utilizing personalized content notice a considerably richer information experience. Contextually furnishes relevant information with refreshing clarity and accuracy for discovery and findability. With all these advantages, investing in a content personalization strategy will benefit your organization. Your customers and employees will also thank you."

—Chip Gettinger, VP of Global Solutions Consulting, RWS

"It's hard to believe that 25 years ago XML was in its infancy. Most industries had not yet started with any kind of structuring, and even the use of email was not that common. Like Scriptorium, Data Conversion Laboratory (DCL) has watched in amazement at the rapid pace of change in content standards and methodologies needed to facilitated content transformation. And it's not slowing —we're collecting knowledge and information faster than ever, and supporting enterprises' content strategy with industry standard formats, technology, and industry-leading tools is more important than ever. Looking in wonder at the last 25, I can't even imagine where we'll be 25 years from now, but it's going to be exciting."

—Mark Gross, President, Data Conversion Laboratory (DCL)

"Content powers business. It enables the lightning of human thought to be captured in a bottle and makes personal conversations between organisations and users possible across time and space. Do everything you can to learn to optimise it. Scriptorium can help."

—Noz Urbina, Principal, Urbina Consulting & Founder, OmnichannelX

Acknowledgments

This book is a collection of Scriptorium articles covering topics such as structured content, content strategy, content operations, and more.

Content authors

- Sarah O'Keefe
- Alan Pringle
- Bill Swallow
- Gretyl Kinsey

Graphics

- Gretyl Kinsey

Cover design

- Jeff Crawford

Book design

- Simon Bate
- Jake Campbell
- Melissa Kershes

Project lead

- Elizabeth Patterson

Project support

- Edwin Skau

Special thanks to Patrick Bosek, Rahel Bailie, Carlos Evia, Jeffrey MacIntyre, Kevin Nichols, and Divraj Singh for sharing ideas and conversations that helped us clarify our thinking when writing The Content Ops Manifesto and Content as a Service (CaaS).

Foreword

A quarter-century business milestone mandates reflection. First, we are grateful for all of you—the community of professionals that has sustained and supported us. Second, it's striking what has and has not changed.

We established Scriptorium to address a simple question: How can we use technology to improve content and publishing? In the beginning, this meant efficiency gains and removing wasted effort from the workflow. These days, we are more focused on increasing the value of content and improving customer experience. But still, eliminating manual drudgery gives authors more time for great content.

Our digital world demands smart content—information that is structured, tagged, and labeled for machine processing. We are certain that there's still a lot of work to do in this area because we haven't even agreed on its name—is it smart content, semantic content, intelligent content, or structured content?

This book provides a glimpse into Scriptorium's thinking on structured content, content strategy, content operations, and more. We hope you find it useful.

Sarah O'Keefe
Alan Pringle
Bill Swallow

About Scriptorium

Scriptorium delivers content solutions for companies to ensure scalability, globalization, and efficient content operations.

Over the past 25 years, we have worked with clients in finance, life sciences, technology, software, heavy machinery, nuclear power, government, military, education, and more. Our focus is on solving the challenges inherent to producing large amounts of content in multiple formats, variants, and languages.

For more information, visit us at scriptorium.com.

The Scriptorium approach to content strategy

Executive summary

Scriptorium's approach to content strategy is based on management consulting principles. First, we identify business goals that are connected to content problems. We then do a needs analysis and gap analysis, and develop requirements. That work provides the foundation for a recommendation. From that recommendation, we build out the solution.

The key to success is the balance between content and strategy. It's easy to reduce the cost of the content lifecycle if you don't care about the quality of the content. If you focus only on the quality of the end result and not on the content creation process, you can end up with beautifully crafted content that's only usable in a single format, that's impossible to translate, or that takes entirely too long to create.

When you invest in content strategy, you are committing to a major digital transformation effort. The challenges are significant, but so is the opportunity.

Current state analysis

Nearly every organization produces content, but with varying degrees of content quality and process maturity. Our content strategy work begins with an assessment of the current state. Typically, we will do the following:

- Audit existing content.
- Document the content lifecycle.

- Inventory content-related software and tools.

- Interview content stakeholders.

If you focus only on the quality of the end
result and not on the content creation
process, you can end up with beautifully
crafted content that's only usable in a
single format, that's impossible to translate,
or that takes entirely too long to create.

Content audit

The purpose of a content audit is to understand the
content landscape. We want to explore the following
issues:

- *What types of information are available and in what
  formats?* In addition to a core product content group,
  an organization might have a training group that
  produces e-learning content and also printed training
  materials for instructor-led training. To understand
  what is being created and by whom, we look at a cross-
  sample of content types.

- *Is the information accurate and up-to-date?* We look
  for obvious technical errors or cases where the
  information in one document contradicts another. We
  ask the content creators about lag times and customer
  complaints. How do content development cycles affect
  product delivery? How are errors identified and

corrected? What does the review and approval process look like?

- *Is the information appropriate for the target audience?* Does the target audience include a lot of people who are non-native speakers or people with limited reading proficiency? Those groups need simple, clear content with plenty of explanatory images. Videos and other visual content are especially helpful for this group. If the audience is subject matter experts, industry shorthand may be appropriate. We also ask some questions about delivery formats. Is the organization delivering in the formats that the audience prefers? Is the information in the right language for the target audience?

- *Does the information connect the reader with additional resources?* Does a troubleshooting procedure list required parts, and are those parts easy to locate? Does a conceptual overview provide additional reading? Does a training overview point readers to the product content where they can find additional in-depth information?

- *Is there appropriate personalization?* Complex products may allow or even require customers to choose different feature sets. Based on a customer profile, you could deliver personalized content that includes only relevant features or that tailors the level of detail to the reader's experience level.

- *How many total pages of content does the organization have and in which languages?* A major multinational corporation may sell hundreds of products and manage more than 50,000 pages of content. Contrast that with a small software startup that needs 500 pages or less to describe a single product.

Content lifecycle

The content lifecycle is the process by which information is created, managed, reviewed, published, translated, and eventually deleted. Some organizations have documented processes for the content lifecycle; most organizations do not. But in every organization, there are unwritten assumptions and established ways of getting the job done.

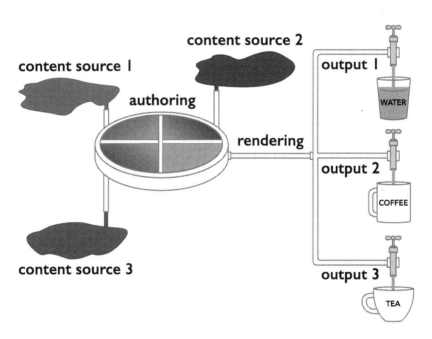

To assess the content lifecycle, we look at the following factors:

- *Longevity.* When a piece of content is created, how long is it available? Does it expire or go out of date? If so, what triggers expiration?

- *Governance.* Who decides when content is ready for publication? Who decides when content should be deleted? How do you decide to create new content?

- *Process.* What processes does a piece of content go through from concept to publication to archiving? Do different types of content go through different processes? If so, what are the criteria that determine content categories?

- *Risk.* What makes content high risk or low risk? Can using this content affect anyone's health and safety? Are there legal or regulatory risks?

Software inventory

The software inventory focuses on the tools and technologies that your organization is using throughout the content lifecycle. Often, that means Word for authoring, and PDF for review and distribution. But even a straightforward Word-based content development environment probably includes supporting tools for graphics. We also look for connected software and systems. During the software inventory, we find a huge variety of systems, often including the following:

- Word processor and desktop publishing tools

- Help authoring tools

- Web development tools

- Content management systems
- Wikis
- Knowledge management systems
- Graphic software packages (for screen shots, CAD, and illustrations)
- Video, animation, and software simulation software
- Audio capture software
- E-learning software
- Learning management systems
- Learning content management systems
- Software code (with embedded comments and string files for software interface text)
- Database software (for parts lists and product specifications)
- Spreadsheets
- Source control systems
- Site generation systems
- Translation management systems
- Translation memory systems

Interviewing stakeholders

Every organization has content stakeholders. The most obvious stakeholders are the content creators and the content consumers, but there are many others who have some responsibility for content. We interview stakeholders to ferret out the undocumented assumptions about content. A typical list includes the following roles and functions:

- Content authors (in technical communication, marketing communication, training, technical support, and more)
- Content reviewers and approvers
- Product managers
- IT
- Technical support (often the biggest internal content consumer and also a likely content creator)
- Risk management
- Legal
- Safety
- Localization
- Field service and service technicians

Gap analysis

From the current state analysis, we can do a gap analysis. The gap analysis spells out the problems with the current state.

Typical gaps include content that:

- Doesn't match corporate branding, voice, and tone.
- Is not easily searchable.

- Takes many months to localize.

- Is out of date or technically inaccurate.

- Is not appropriate for the target audience.

- Is duplicated in many places.

The gap analysis describes the difference between the desired state and the current state. It is of course tempting to flesh out the gap analysis with solutions or requirements ("content is not easily searchable *because it is locked in huge PDF files*"), but we try to focus the gap analysis on the difference between the desired future state ("customers can easily find the information that they need") and the current state ("customers can't find the information that they need"). The gap analysis gives us an idea of the scope of the problems we need to solve. Multiple gaps might have the same root cause.

Needs analysis

During the needs analysis, we look at the identified gaps and describe how to change things to reach the desired state. For example:

- *Improve search:* need to deliver content in search-friendly HTML topics instead of a single PDF file

- *Speed up localization:* need to change the localization process to deliver localized content in 2–4 weeks rather than six months or more

- *Improve technical accuracy:* rework the content review and approval process

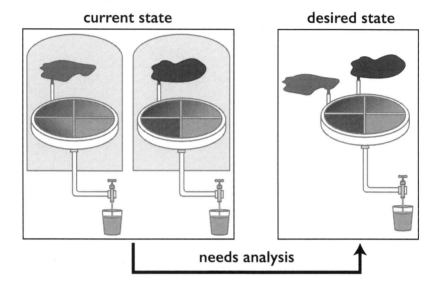

The outcome of the needs analysis is a set of high-level requirements, such as "ensure content is usable on multiple devices," "create a style guide so that writers create content with a unified voice," or "build an enterprise taxonomy."

Recommendation

When we recommend a content strategy solution to a customer, our goal is to find the best way to turn the requirements into reality. The challenge here is that, in addition to content requirements, we often have additional business requirements, such as limited funding, external regulatory requirements, or a focus on risk reduction. The size of the company, the type of content, and the company culture all play important parts in shaping the recommendation.

Our content strategy asssessments typically include the following components:

- Content model and information architecture.

- Reuse, localization, and conversion strategies.

- Software recommendations for authoring, reviewing, and delivering content.

- Business case, which provides a discussion of how the new strategy will improve business outcomes. The most common driver is cost reduction or cost avoidance, but we also look for opportunities to increase revenue and for more qualitative goals, like improved user experience or better alignment with brand positioning. We have to be able to justify the proposed investment—and the risk of making changes —by showing a significant return on investment to the business.

- Implementation overview, which provides a high-level project plan for the tasks that need to be completed to execute the recommended strategy along with an estimated cost.

Scriptorium's Content Ops Manifesto

Content Operations (Content Ops) is the engine that drives your content lifecycle.

Scriptorium's Content Ops Manifesto describes the four basic principles of content operations.

1. Semantic content is the foundation

2. Friction is expensive

3. Emphasize availability

4. Plan for change

Semantic content is the foundation

Single-channel publishing processes, where content is written, edited, and then sent to a specific output type, are obsolete. Instead, content is pushed, pulled, assembled, disassembled, and manipulated for many different targets.

To accommodate these diverse requirements, the content needs to carry contextual information, such as:

- *Tags.* Tags are identifying information, such as *title, abstract, link,* or *emphasis.*

- *Metadata.* Metadata provides additional information. For example, you might have a *booktitle* tag with *isbn* metadata. The *booktitle* tag gives you the common name of the book, but the *isbn* metadata identifies the exact edition and could be used to create a link to an online bookseller or database. At a higher level, metadata lets you classify information, such as by subject matter, author, or product family. A classification system lets you sort and filter information.

- *Sequencing and hierarchy.* To assemble small chunks of content into a larger document, you need sequencing and hierarchy information. For example, a magazine is made up of a collection of articles. To generate a print version of the magazine, you need to specify the order of the articles. A document hierarchy lets you define a tree relationship among pieces of content. For example, an article might include several sidebars, and those sidebars are considered subordinate to the main article. You need a way to capture sequencing and hierarchy information for different types of content.

Friction is expensive

In a content lifecycle, friction refers to productivity impediments—processes that require human intervention:

- Copying and pasting information from one location to another
- Manual formatting (or reformatting) of content to accommodate different delivery channels or languages
- Manual collaboration, review, and approval workflows
- Process workarounds to address special one-off requirements
- Creating redundant copies of information instead of using existing content

A sufficient degree of friction in the content lifecycle makes it impossible to scale up content. For example, consider a marketing white paper. The plan is to publish the white paper on the company website in HTML and PDF formats. In addition, the marketing team will use excerpts from the white paper in promotional emails and tweets. The document will also be translated into 10 languages to support the company's global audience.

Eliminate friction so that you can operate more efficiently and more accurately.

Here are some common points of friction and ways to eliminate them:

- White paper is published in HTML and then converted into PDF by hand. Avoid this by authoring the content in a neutral format and then automatically converting it to HTML and PDF.

- Marketing team reads through white paper to identify key points to use in emails and tweets. Instead, have the white paper author tag key points in the source documents and extract the tagged content automatically. For the emails, pull out the document's tagged title and abstract.

- HTML is translated and then re-converted into PDF for all 10 languages. To avoid this, ship the neutral format for translation and make sure that the automatic conversion to HTML and PDF supports all the required languages.

- Authors duplicating existing information. To attack redundancy, set up a content management system that helps authors find usable chunks of information and reuse them as needed.

Content scalability[1] refers to your ability to expand your content lifecycle to process more content, more content types, more channels, more languages, and more variants. The greater your scalability needs, the more critical it becomes to eliminate friction.

---

[1] https://www.scriptorium.com/2021/05/content-scalability-removing-friction-from-your-content-lifecycle/

Workflow and governance[2] are also common areas of friction. In some industries, complex approval workflows and multiple layers of quality control are necessary. But many organizations have time-consuming, multifaceted governance processes that don't match the risk profile of the content. If your content is regulated, can have health and safety risks, or is otherwise high risk, heavy governance may be needed.

Friction slows down your content lifecycle and introduces waste into the process. Eliminate it so that you can operate more efficiently and more accurately. Software tools, especially content management systems, translation management systems, and automated rendering engines, are essential components

Emphasize availability

Customers expect content on demand, in their preferred format and language. For content ops, that means focusing on content access:

- *Ensure that information is current and accurate.* Push updates early and often.

- *Ensure that information is accessible.* Do not assume that all of your readers have perfect vision, hearing, and fine motor control. Instead, provide at least two ways to access information—at a minimum, a podcast should have a transcript, a graphic should have a

---

[2] https://www.scriptorium.com/2021/08/establishing-content-governance/

descriptive caption, and videos should have captions. Provide keyboard navigation options in addition to clickable regions. Choose colors carefully, so that a color-blind person can use your material.

- *Provide a variety of delivery options to accommodate your customer's needs.* Consider how you might improve the customer experience with personalized information delivery.

- *Give customers entry points into the information:* for example, search, faceted search, filtering, category-based navigation, linking related information, and curated pages for specific topics.

- *Localize and translate your content.* Remember that in many countries, you will need more than one language to reach your target audience. The US, for example, has roughly 40 million native Spanish speakers.

- In addition to traditional content publishing (the organization pushes out content for users), *look at a pull model*, in which a user can request relevant information from a repository.

- *Consider the user's context* in time and space to improve the relevance of information.

Plan for change

Content ops will evolve with new forms of content, new tools, and new business requirements. With this in mind, prioritize flexibility:

- When you choose a platform, have an exit strategy in mind from the beginning.

- Audit your systems regularly to ensure that they are still meeting your needs.

- Conduct forward-looking needs analysis to identify emerging trends and requirements.

- Build out metrics and measurements that help you understand your content ops systems' overall performance.

Content accounting
Calculating the value of content in the enterprise

The challenge of content value

Content value is a hot topic in marketing and technical communication. In the publishing industry, the connection between content and value is clear. A publisher sells a book (or film or other piece of content) and gets book sales, ticket revenue, or streaming subscriptions in return. But what if your content is a part of the product (like user documentation) or used to sell the product (like a marketing white paper)? In these cases, measuring content value is much more challenging.

It is tempting to fall back on measuring cost instead of value. The cost of content development can be a trap, though. Eliminating wasted effort and optimizing content workflows is sensible, but too much focus on cost leads us toward content as a commodity.

Content should not be treated as a commodity. Good content:

- Persuades people to choose a specific product
- Enables people to understand complex technical concepts
- Reduces product returns
- Helps people use products correctly and thereby avoid injuries or costly errors
- Eliminates the need for a call to technical support
- Burnishes a company's reputation

Good content delivers business value.

This white paper proposes a framework for measuring content value based on accounting principles.

Accounting principles

Financial accounting starts with two basic documents: a profit and loss statement (P&L) and a balance sheet.

The P&L shows income and expenses over time. For content accounting purposes, the expense side is straightforward—it lists salaries, rent payments, and other costs. The income side shows payments from customers for products and services. A content-focused company can align income (for example, book sales or a website subscription) with the expenses (such as salaries for writers, website infrastructure, editing expenses, and printing expenses).

Profit & Loss: publishing company

INCOME		
Textbook sales	$	1,000,000
E-learning courses	$	500,000
TOTAL INCOME	**$**	**1,500,000**
EXPENSES		
Content creation	$	800,000
Printing	$	400,000
TOTAL EXPENSES	**$**	**1,200,000**
NET INCOME	$	300,000

Simplified P&L for a publishing company

The balance sheet lists assets, liabilities, and equity. Assets minus liabilities always equals equity. The best-understood example of this is a house. If you own a house worth $250,000 and have a $200,000 mortgage, then your equity is $50,000.

Balance sheet

ASSETS		
My house	$	250,000
TOTAL ASSETS	**$**	**250,000**
LIABILITIES		
Mortgage	$	200,000
TOTAL LIABILITIES	**$**	**200,000**
EQUITY		
Equity	$	50,000
TOTAL LIABILITIES & EQUITY	**$**	**250,000**

Simplified balance sheet for a homeowner

In a business context, assets are items that have long-term value, such as office buildings and equipment. For a coffee shop, a high-end espresso machine might be listed as an asset. Many organizations also include the value of intellectual property, especially if they hold a patent. Liabilities include bills that need to be paid and long-term debt. Organizations may also list expected liabilities, such as anticipated product returns or legal liabilities due to product defects.

In an organization where content plays a supporting role, content *expenses* are usually measured, but not content-related income, assets, or liabilities.

Creating a content P&L

To create a content-focused P&L, you need to measure income and expenses related to content.

Income

To measure income, we have chosen to focus on contributions based on a hierarchy of business needs.

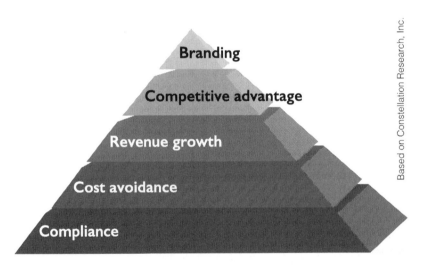

Hierarchy of business needs

Compliance

If your company is regulated, compliance is a key reason that you have content. Unless you deliver the content required by regulators, you cannot sell the product. Some industries where compliance is important include:

- *Pharmaceuticals and life sciences:* Drug labels and material safety data sheets must follow formats specified by the U.S. FDA and other regulatory agencies. Medical device documentation is also regulated.

- *Heavy machinery:* Operating instructions for industrial equipment sold in the European Union are regulated by the EU's machinery directive.

- *Insurance and finance:* Insurance policies must meet different requirements in each state in the U.S. Financial documents may require specific formats and contents.

Producing documents that meet compliance requirements is a cost of doing business. Without compliant content, the organization cannot participate in the market.

Cost avoidance

In content workflows, we can reduce costs in several ways:

- *Efficiency:* To improve efficiency, we look for ways to squeeze out waste from the content development process. One common area for improvement is review workflows—reducing the number of people who review content, ensuring that reviews are focused, and providing for concurrent instead of serial reviews.

- *Reuse:* For technical content especially, reuse is a powerful way to reduce costs. Reuse means less total content to maintain, which in turn reduces the overall cost of ownership and downstream localization costs.

- *Automation:* Formatting automation is another powerful way to reduce the overall cost of content development. An upfront investment in publishing software can result in eliminating 30–50% of recurring content development efforts.[3]

Efficiency, reuse, and automation are typically used to justify an investment in publishing software or improved workflows. Cost avoidance doesn't create additional income, but it does mean increased productivity.

OLD SYSTEM			NEW SYSTEM		
Content creation	$	8,000,000	Content creation		$ 6,400,000
Software	$	40,000	Software		$ 1,000,000
Localization	$	2,000,000	Localization		$ 1,600,000
TOTAL EXPENSES	**$**	**10,040,000**	**TOTAL EXPENSES**		**$ 9,000,000**

Cost avoidance via software investment

In addition to a systems argument, consider a few additional possibilities for cost avoidance:

- *Product liability:* Especially in the United States, legal liability is a concern. Injuries resulting from use or misuse of a product can be reduced or avoided by providing better content. This in return reduces the company's legal exposure (and uninjured customers tend to be happier customers). Reuse helps ensure

---

[3] Industry estimates are that writers working in Microsoft Word spend 30–50% of their total time on formatting. Moving to systems that separate content and formatting eliminates that formatting time.

that all content is current and accurate, thus reducing potential liability.

- *Product returns:* One rough estimate is that $17B are lost annually due to product returns of consumer electronics.[4] Up to 20% of these returns are because customers cannot understand how to use a product, as opposed to an actually defective product. Improve product content to reduce the rate of product returns.

- *Technical support costs:* Technical support calls are one-to-one, and staffing call centers is complex. By contrast, an article that answers a common question is written once and then consumed by many customers. Investing in useful, searchable technical support content is usually less expensive than providing live technical support.

Revenue growth

Content can drive revenue growth. To support revenue growth, consider the following:

- *Content marketing:* Invest in useful persuasive content to spread the word about your organization's product. Improve the reach of your content with search engine optimization.

- *Localization:* To broaden global reach, invest in local languages. In a Common Sense Advisory research survey, 75% of respondents agreed or strongly agreed

---

[4] https://www.chainstoreage.com/operations/this-is-why-so-many-non-defective-consumer-electronics-products-are-returned/

that "When faced with the choice of buying two similar products, I am more likely to purchase the one that has product information in my language."[5]

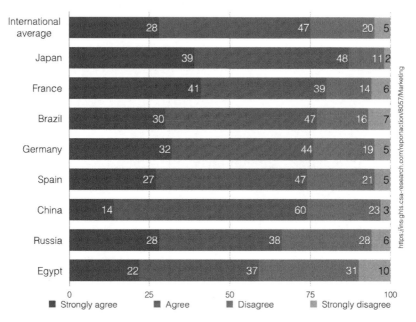

Survey question: "When faced with the choice of buying two similar products, I am more likely to purchase the one that has product information in my language." (source: Common Sense Advisory)

- *Improve product content:* Better product content means fewer product returns (discussed in cost avoidance), better reviews, and happier customers. All of these factors contribute to repeat business and market share growth.

---

[5] https://insights.csa-research.com/reportaction/8057/Marketing

Competitive advantage

Beyond good search, SEO, and localization, content can provide a direct competitive advantage. For an example, consider King Arthur Flour, which sells a variety of flours. King Arthur Flour does well on a basic Google search for "flour," but they are in a sea of other possibilities. But someone at the company went deeper. Many people in their target audience are baking from scratch. To improve baking results, flour should be measured by weight rather than volume. So as a baker, a common search would be "how much does flour weigh." And here, you see that King Arthur Flour owns the results.

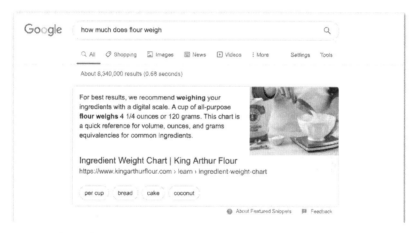

King Arthur Flour gets the coveted featured snippet and the first result for "how much does flour weigh" (2019)

The link takes the reader to a handy chart that lists weights for several different flour varieties. So King Arthur has now captured the attention of potential customers.

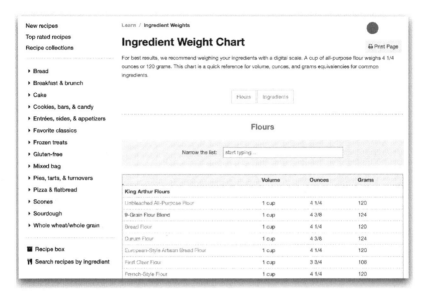

The ingredient weight chart

Branding

Your content can contribute the overall company brand identity. Marketing, technical, and product content can all support the company's brand. A prestige brand needs to have content that supports premium position. A product with friendly, informal positioning (such as the Slack messaging platform) needs content that matches.

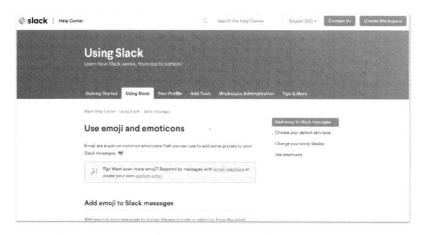

The help content uses Slack branding, both in appearance and in tone

Expenses

Most organizations have a good understanding of the content creation expenses. These include:

• Employee salaries and related costs

• Facilities

• Software

• Travel

• Education

If you do not have access to these costs within your organization, a reasonable estimate is $100/hour for content creators in North America. (That amount assumes a staff employee and includes benefits and all additional expenses.)

Based on a loaded hourly cost, you can work out the total cost of staff. For contractors and vendors, use the amounts on their invoices.

Creating a content balance sheet

A balance sheet lists assets and liabilities. In general accounting, an asset is something that has long-term value, either cash or something that can be converted into cash, like real estate. A liability is a debt, such as a bank loan or an outstanding credit card balance.

Assets

For your balance sheet, you need to measure the value of content assets that have long-term value to the business, including:

- Content, such as white papers, product content, and other in-depth information
- Content management systems and output pipelines
- Content development assets, such as glossaries, terminology standards, and style guidelines
- Content taxonomies
- Content models
- Localization assets, especially translation memory and multilingual terminology
- Localization management systems and output pipelines

We also need to think about depreciation—the idea that an asset can lose its value over time. A car, for example, starts out with a certain value. After 10 years, the car is worth a lot less than it was when it was first purchased. Most content assets also depreciate—after a few years, a white paper is out of date. So the content balance sheet needs to be updated periodically to capture the change in value for the various assets.

Here are some factors that affect content value:

- Accuracy
- Relevance
- Targeted to the right audience
- Useful to the targeted audience
- Accomplishes its purpose (for example, describes a product's features and benefits or explains a concept)
- Longevity
- Localization-friendly

Certain factors serve as content value multipliers:

- Reuse: Is the content used in multiple locations?
- Content variants: Does the content enable you to create multiple versions from a single source?
- Multichannel output: Can the content be delivered to multiple output formats automatically?
- Is there a localized version of this content in your repository?

Liabilities

Liabilities reduce the value of your content. Your liabilities are content debt—the work that needs to be done to bring your content up to the needed standard (or to create it).[6] They include the following:

- *Bad content experience:* The information is unattractive, hard to understand, and/or inaccessible.

- *Out of date:* The information needs to be updated.

- *Wrong audience:* The information is targeted at the wrong audience. For example, a document intended for patients in a hospital uses complex medical terminology that only medical professionals would understand.

- *Wrong voice and tone:* The information does not meet the organization's standards for voice and tone. For example, a casual game company would likely use informal language, so a formal, legalistic document would be the wrong voice and tone.

- *Offensive:* The information uses offensive language or stereotypes.

- *Wrong format:* The information does not use the format preferred by the consumer of the information.

- *Badly translated:* The information is available in the target languages, but the translation is poor, so it leaves the reader with a bad impression.

---

[6] https://18f.gsa.gov/2016/05/19/content-debt-what-it-is-where-to-find-it-and-how-to-prevent-it-in-the-first-place/

Putting it all together

So at this point, you can put together your first content accounting reports.

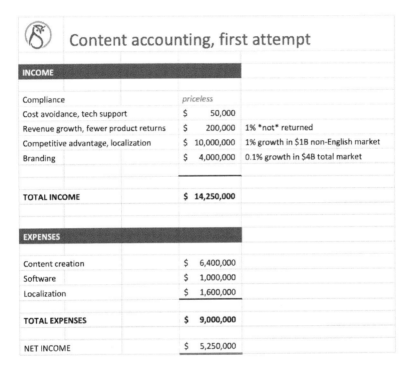

Content accounting, first attempt		
INCOME		
Compliance	*priceless*	
Cost avoidance, tech support	$ 50,000	
Revenue growth, fewer product returns	$ 200,000	1% *not* returned
Competitive advantage, localization	$ 10,000,000	1% growth in $1B non-English market
Branding	$ 4,000,000	0.1% growth in $4B total market
TOTAL INCOME	$ 14,250,000	
EXPENSES		
Content creation	$ 6,400,000	
Software	$ 1,000,000	
Localization	$ 1,600,000	
TOTAL EXPENSES	$ 9,000,000	
NET INCOME	$ 5,250,000	

Content accounting P&L

Content balance sheet, first attempt

ASSETS		
Content assets	$ 10,000,000	
Content system	$ 500,000	CMS and output pipelines
Localization assets	$ 2,000,000	
Localization system	$ 250,000	TMS and output pipelines
TOTAL ASSETS	**$ 12,750,000**	
LIABILITIES		
Bad content	$ 1,000,000	wrong, out-of-date
Content debt	$ 1,000,000	missing content
Bad localization	$ 1,000,000	wrong, badly translated
Localization debt	$ 3,000,000	missing content
TOTAL LIABILITIES	**$ 6,000,000**	
EQUITY		
Equity	$ 6,750,000	
TOTAL LIABILITIES & EQUITY	**$ 12,750,000**	

Content accounting balance sheet

The DITA
business case
Maximizing content value

Executive summary

Companies require content to support ever-increasing requirements, including:

- Delivering content in multiple formats
- Meeting compliance requirements
- Accelerating time to market
- Handling content variants
- Delivering translated content on a limited budget

This white paper describes the business justifications for investing in the Darwin Information Typing Architecture (DITA)—an open source XML standard—as a foundation for content management.

Need for information in multiple formats

DITA XML files are encoded in plain text markup that looks similar to HTML. From DITA XML, you can render content into many formats, including PDF, HTML, Word, Markdown, InDesign, man pages, JSON, WordPress, and SCORM. Each publishing pipeline can also be set up to support multiple languages. Once you configure the publishing pipeline, the process of generating output is automated.

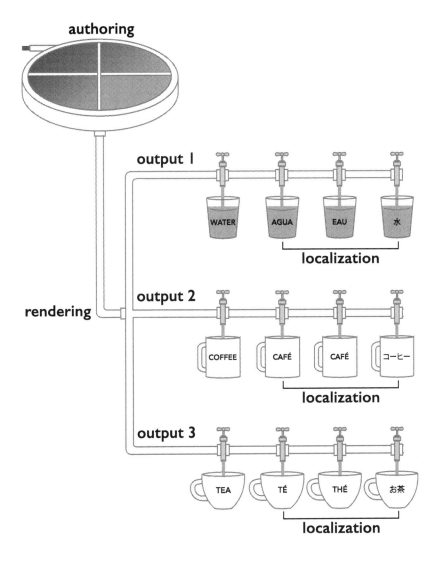

Automation can provide the following benefits:

- Your organization can ensure that all information streams are in sync.

- Instead of repetitive manual processes to set up and format each content delivery type, you configure the publishing pipeline once and then let it run.

- In a well-designed pipeline, the changes required for localization are isolated into configuration files, which makes it straightforward to add new languages or make adjustments for a specific language.

- Starting from XML gives you the flexibility to add new content delivery formats as needed.

- You can integrate the publishing pipeline into other enterprise tools, such as source control, QA, and build systems, to further automate the content updates.

Compliance requirements

DITA is useful to ensure compliance with regulatory and legal frameworks. The DITA content model is configurable, and you can validate content against the required model. You can use DITA validation to ensure that the document you are submitting contains the required information, in the specified order. Editors can then concentrate on the quality of the text rather than double-checking the technical compliance against the document standard.

For example, you can set up a DITA content model for a medical journal article to require an abstract, author information including credentials and affiliations, and required content containers in a specified order (introduction, method, results, and discussion, for example). Without these required components, the article is not valid. An editor would read the abstract to ensure that it is an accurate representation of the article.

You can configure DITA to require, allow, and disallow content components in different contexts. Inside DITA tools, authors have guided editing; the software tells them which elements are required and allowed at different points in a document.

Accelerating time to market

DITA can improve content velocity (time to market) in the following ways:

- Content reuse means less content to manage. Content is written once and then referenced into multiple other locations.

- Automated formatting means less authoring effort and faster delivery of content, in all languages.

- Connected content. You can extract information from its source and automatically push it into the DITA content. For example, you can extract product specifications from an engineering product database instead of copying and pasting. If the database is updated, the document changes accordingly.

In addition to efficiency in your publishing workflow, you can also assess reduced time to market and how the earlier availability of product content might affect product delivery. If a product sells a modest $1 million per year, then each week of availability is worth about $20,000. If you can deliver your content sooner and thereby accelerate the delivery of the product or reduce the delays in shipping localized versions, you can potentially get your revenue faster.

The most common business case for accelerated time to market is in reducing the wait for localized content.

Supporting content variants

Variants allow you to eliminate content redundancy and provide targeted information to support product variants (for example, product models with both shared and different features). This strategy can also help you meet customer requirements for personalized documentation.

In DITA, you can set up content variants with multiple facets, such as platform, customer, audience, and product. This allows you to create a huge number of possible variants from a single set of source files. You can then use the tagged content to publish each variant or support a dynamic versioning approach.

Localization cost savings

If you localize your content, DITA can streamline the translation and formatting work:

- *Translation effort:* DITA offers a robust content reuse framework. Instead of copying and pasting reusable text, the content is written only once and is included by reference as needed. This means that the text is also translated once (per language), regardless of how often it appears in the published content. Reducing the total number of words translated is a powerful way to reduce the overall cost of localization. In addition, it improves the quality of the information by ensuring consistency throughout the document. (After information is copied and pasted, copies inexorably diverge over time.)

- *Formatting costs:* Typically, 30–50 percent of total localization cost in a traditional workflow is for formatting. After the files are translated from the source language into the target language, the files must be reformatted to accommodate text expansion and pagination changes. In a DITA workflow, that formatting is automated. The DITA content files do not contain formatting information. To generate final formatted content, you apply formatting stylesheets to the translated DITA files. These stylesheets are configured ahead of time to support the languages you need. An organization that spends $1,000,000 per year on localization will save $300,000–$500,000 of that amount by eliminating formatting costs.

The DITA ecosystem

DITA adoption has grown steadily since its public debut. The types of companies employing DITA for their content have also grown beyond software to include life sciences, manufacturing, financial, and more. Although DITA has its roots in product and technical content, organizations are also using it for marketing, training, and other important customer-facing content. As a result, there are numerous DITA software vendors. Many organizations use a DITA-specific content management system (CMS) to manage their files. In addition to typical file management, a DITA CMS typically provides:

- Workflows for authoring, editing, approval, and publishing

- Robust search and "where-used" reporting

- Lightweight authoring environments for part-time content contributors

- An Application Programming Interface (API) for connecting to other systems

An API typically allows you to share and retrieve content from other enterprise systems, such as those for asset management, web content, and source control.

Managing DITA projects
Five keys to success

Executive summary

You just completed a content strategy analysis. Your analysis concludes that the Darwin Information Typing Architecture (DITA) XML standard will provide a great framework for your company's content. You are ready to set up a DITA system, but where do you start?

Implementing DITA is not just a matter of picking tools. In fact, software selection is usually the easiest part of a DITA project. This white paper describes best practices for five critical facets of a DITA project.

Ensuring clear communication

Managing change is critical for your DITA project's success. Clear communication through all phases of the project is *the* essential component for successful change management.

Good content addresses its audience at the right level. Take the same approach when communicating with the different groups affected by a DITA implementation.

Talk to project stakeholders about their concerns and requirements in language they understand.

Executives who approve projects will care little about authoring solutions. They are much more interested in finishing the project within budget and reaping the benefits of the DITA system as soon as possible.

For example, occasional content contributors (such as product engineers) need reassurance that they can contribute content quickly and easily, perhaps through a browser-based interface. Full-time content contributors, however, want an XML authoring tool with many features. The IT department does not want to support tools that have the same features, so they need to understand the business reasons for providing two authoring experiences. Executives who approve projects will care little about authoring solutions. They are much more interested in finishing the project within budget and reaping the benefits of the DITA system as soon as possible.

To ensure success, align your DITA project with other strategic projects and how they are managed in your organization. Have regular status meetings during implementation, and communicate with stakeholders through the channels they prefer. (If an executive requests a presentation on project status, sending just an email is not a good idea.)

Even with an excellent DITA system in place, the communication must continue as you roll out the environment and train users. Targeted training should educate casual users, power users, and administrators in separate sessions.

Encourage new users to provide feedback on trouble spots so that you can make needed adjustments. User feedback will also help improve training for the next group of employees.

Content modeling

Even though you have chosen the DITA standard as your XML model, you still need to work through the process of *content modeling:* determining how the organization and classification of your company's information will be represented within DITA.

You can start by creating an inventory of styles for your current authoring tool. Then, list out the DITA equivalents for those styles. Seeing how existing information works in DITA is a good way to learn the DITA structures.

However, do not focus exclusively on how you created content in the past. You may not have followed DITA best practices in your old content (for example, creating small chunks of modular content that you can reuse and share). To develop high-quality DITA content, you may need to change or completely rewrite content.

You also need to figure out how to track *metadata*—data about your data. In DITA, you can use metadata in many ways, including:

- Filtering what content is included or excluded in a publication (conditional text)
- Refining searches
- Including processing instructions for delivery formats (for example, the IDs for context-sensitive help)

There are other content modeling considerations. Do you need additional structures and metadata to fully support your content requirements? A selling point of DITA is the ability to modify the default structure without deviating from the standard. You create new structures based on existing ones through the process of *specialization*.[7]

DITA also offers several mechanisms for content reuse. During the content modeling process, develop a formal content reuse strategy.

---

[7] White paper on specialization: scriptorium.com/2017/10/dita-specialization-extensibility-and-standards-compliance/

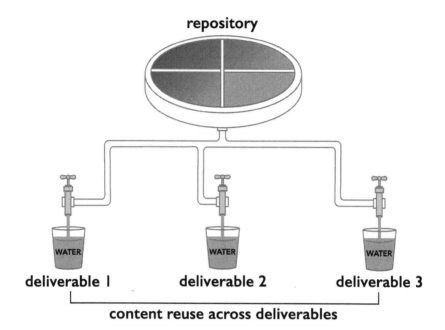

repository

deliverable 1   **deliverable 2**   **deliverable 3**

content reuse across deliverables

Evaluating tools

As you sift through cheery marketing claims for DITA tools, go back to your initial content strategy analysis. You chose DITA to meet specific business requirements. While evaluating software, stay focused on those requirements. Your shopping list may include a component content management system, authoring tools, review tools, a translation management system, and more.

Avoid using your current tools' capabilities as benchmarks for new tools, particularly when moving from desktop publishing to XML. Desktop publishing and XML environments have different authoring experiences, so direct feature-to-feature tool comparisons are not useful. For example, the ease with which authors insert page and line breaks in their desktop publishing program is irrelevant—in a DITA environment, formatting is not applied during the authoring process. Instead, an automated transformation process formats the content later.

Because of different stakeholder requirements, you may need multiple tools for a single task, particularly for authoring. Part-time and full-time content contributors require different levels of complexity in authoring tool features, so it may be more efficient to provide multiple authoring experiences in your DITA workflow.

Create a spreadsheet with weighted requirements so that important tool features get priority during evaluation. You can also develop short narratives that explain specific use cases. Ask each vendor to demonstrate how their tool supports those use cases.

Evaluate vendor claims carefully. If you have identified specific DITA constructs as critical to your workflow (reuse methods, for example), ensure that vendors' demonstrations show how their tools support those DITA features.

Independent consultants such as Scriptorium are experienced in developing requirements and evaluating vendors. An investment in a consultant can result in better decisions.

Delivering content

You can transform your DITA XML content into web pages, PDF files, and other formats through the DITA Open Toolkit.[8] The Open Toolkit is not the only way to publish your DITA content. Other DITA tools provide additional publishing mechanisms.

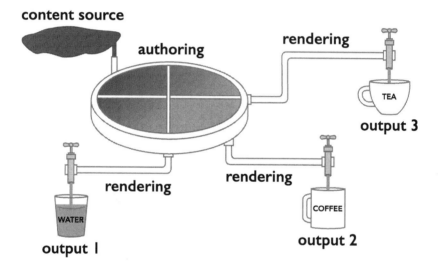

The default formatting from the Open Toolkit is very unattractive, but you can modify the look and feel to match your company's corporate style.

The good news is that once you have the customized transforms in place, it's a quick, pushbutton process to create the delivery formats from the DITA source files. You can also set up automated batch processing so updated output is generated at regular intervals.

---

[8] Download the DITA Open Toolkit for free at www.dita-ot.org.

The toolkit's output capabilities are extensible. For example, Scriptorium has developed transformations for EPUB ebooks, Android applications, InDesign-compatible XML, and much more.

Considering conversion

Before you think about converting your existing content to DITA XML, research DITA best practices. The DITA specification itself contains limited best-practice guidelines. [9] Supplement your research in the specification with a reference such as *The DITA Style Guide* that offers advice on how to implement the DITA model. [10]

If your content is not tagged consistently, it is more difficult to automate conversion through scripts—whether you have an internal resource for the scripting or you work with a conversion vendor. Also, if your content is not easily broken into chunks that are the equivalent of DITA topics, you may need to rewrite it.

Even if you are not going to convert existing information to DITA, you still need content to test your DITA model and the delivery transforms. Create a collection of DITA files that represents the types of content you create and distribute. Collect enough content to ensure you are thoroughly testing your processes and transformations.

---

[9] DITA specification: docs.oasis-open.org/dita/dita/v1.3/dita-v1.3-part3-all-inclusive.html

[10] You can read *The DITA Style Guide* for free at www.oxygenxml.com/dita/styleguide/webhelp-feedback.

Be prepared to address complications during your conversion project (for example, poor tagging or odd layout in a subset of files). Leave ample time in your schedule to address those issues.

Personalized content
Steps to success

More customers are demanding personalized content, and your organization needs a plan to deliver it. But where do you start? How do you assess where personalization should fit into your content lifecycle? How do you coordinate your efforts to ensure that personalization is consistent across the enterprise? This white paper explains what steps you can take to execute a successful personalization strategy.

What is personalization?

Personalization is the delivery of custom, curated information tailored to an individual user's needs. Some of those needs might include:

- Owning a product or product line

- Requiring training on some aspects of product functionality

- Occupying a designated role (such as administrator, editor, author, etc.)

- Having a certain level of experience (such as beginner, intermediate, or expert)

- Living in a specific geographic location (categorized by country or region)

- Speaking a particular language, which may or may not be tied to location

When you personalize, instead of providing all customers with the same content, you provide individual customers with only the content they need based on these and other factors.

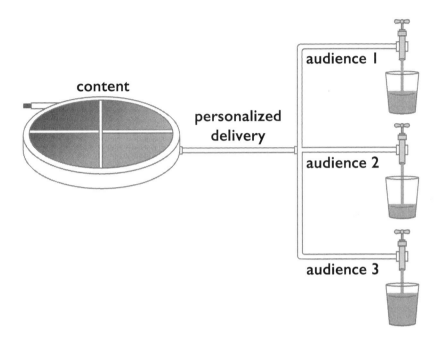

Personalized delivery methods

Personalized content can be delivered in the following ways:

- *Author-controlled personalization:* content creators develop subsets of the content intended for different segments of the audience
- *User-controlled personalization:* users filter the content to the subset they need by selecting facets that apply to them

- *System-controlled personalization:* a delivery platform automatically delivers the relevant content based on information contained in each user's profile

Your company may choose one of these approaches or a combination depending on what your customers demand. In all cases, it helps to maintain the content in a semantically rich structure. This allows authors to tag the content according to the ways it should be divided and distributed to customers.

Author-controlled personalization

Content with author-controlled personalization can be delivered in both print-based and digital formats. Examples might include:

- Creating user-specific training modules from hand-picked sets of lessons

- Publishing a subset of chapters from a user manual as a custom document

- Tailoring presentations on what's new in your products to each specific audience

Typically, author-controlled personalization is managed in one of the following ways:

- Authors sort out the relevant information from their entire body of content before delivering it to the user

- Authors create one set of common content (which is delivered to all users) and numerous smaller sets of content that are personalized for individuals or groups

User-controlled personalization

With user-controlled personalization, your company hands over the controls to the customers. They can use checkboxes and dropdown menus to help them narrow down your content to the pieces they need. These facets can be used to personalize search results so that customers find the right information more quickly.

To support this functionality, user-controlled personalization requires digital delivery, such as a website, help system, or e-learning environment. The delivery platform must be set up with all the facets a customer might need to find the relevant content.

System-controlled personalization

System-controlled personalization takes user-controlled personalization one step further: instead of requiring customers to narrow down the content manually, the delivery platform serves up custom content automatically based on information in each customer's profile. All customers have to do is log in to access the personalized information they need.

Much like user-controlled personalization, system-controlled personalization also requires digital delivery, typically through a dynamic delivery portal. The portal must be equipped to store and manage user profiles and all the relevant demographics, product history, and other information needed for personalized delivery.

Why personalize your content?

Delivering personalized content can be a challenge, especially if you've never done so before. So what makes it worth the effort?

> "Customers are more likely to remember what they read (or read your content at all!) when they don't have to sift through irrelevant information.

Personalization offers several benefits, including:

- *Better findability.* When customers search a set of personalized content, that means they'll get personalized results. This will make it faster and easier for them to pinpoint the information they need.

- *More satisfied customers.* The easier it is to consume your content, the happier customers will be with the overall experience of using your product. For example, customers who can start by selecting which products they own will have an easier time using the content than those who have to pick through instructions like "If you have product A, do X; if you have product B, do Y." Delivering content that isn't personalized requires extra work from them to find what they need.

- *Fewer support calls.* Customers are more likely to remember what they read (or read your content at all!) when they don't have to sift through irrelevant information. This reduces the volume of support calls your organization receives—and improves the quality of the questions that still come in.

- *Contextually relevant content.* Based on the support calls you do receive, personalization can help you develop more specific content for certain situations (for example, troubleshooting information). That content can then be used to create personalized FAQs and instructions to help your customers further.

All of these benefits can save your organization time and other costs. To determine whether it makes sense to pursue personalization, it's important to assess those savings and estimate your return on investment.

Steps to personalization

Once you have decided to deliver personalized content, you need a plan to achieve that goal. A personalization strategy can help you navigate some of the most common challenges organizations face, such as a large volume of content or a lack of semantic tagging.

The following steps will set you up for successful personalization:

1. Determine the needs

2. Develop the roadmap

3. Prepare the content

4. Support the solution

Determine the needs

The first step in any good content strategy is assessing your current situation to determine what you need, and personalization is no different. Because personalization requires labels in your content to help sort it by different user requirements, a helpful place to start is by looking at the metadata and terminology your company uses. Do you already have a taxonomy[11] in place, and if so, how can you leverage it for personalization?

Personalized content is designed to benefit your customers, so they will also be an important source of information for this part of your plan. Each content producing department should gather feedback and metrics from customers to help answer the following questions:

- How do your customers use your products (and their associated content)?

- What information are they required to know to perform a task using your products?

- Which products are they most likely to buy based on their past purchase history?

- What would make their experience better with using your products?

- How do they search for the information they need, and what challenges do they face in finding it?

---

[11] https://www.scriptorium.com/2015/11/tips-for-developing-a-taxonomy-in-dita/

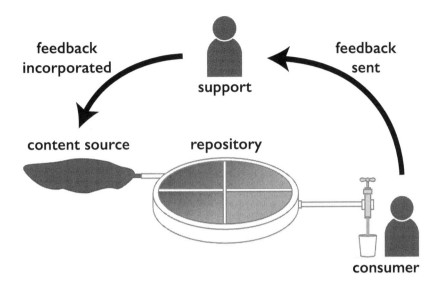

If your organization hasn't been collecting this type of customer information, it's never too late to start. You don't have to collect this data ahead of time—you can ask customers questions like "What is your experience level?" or "Would you like information on product A or B?" when they access your content. You may also be able to get some useful information from your support team, who can tell you what kinds of customer questions and complaints they receive most frequently.

Once you have a solid set of data, compare notes across departments. Do customers have a difficult time finding what they need in the user manuals? Would they respond better to more targeted marketing materials? Are there patterns in your metrics that show similarities among different groups? This analysis will show you where departments can coordinate on an approach to personalization.

Develop the roadmap

Once you've gathered your metrics and used that information to determine your needs, the next step is laying the groundwork by developing a roadmap. The roadmap is a document that captures the details of your personalization strategy and how you will put it in place.

Your personalization roadmap should include:

- A timeline with short-term and long-term goals
- A budget with resource requirements and return on investment
- An analysis of where personalization fits into the content lifecycle, including:
  - Which content you plan to personalize
  - What data you need to collect to do so
  - How you will collect and manage that data
  - How you will apply that data to the content
- A list of needed content development process changes
- A plan for personalization governance

Personalization is most effective when it's a consistent and coordinated effort across the enterprise. Therefore, it's important for departments to use their combined metrics from the previous step to inform the roadmap.

Prepare the content

Once you have your roadmap, the next part of the process is setting up your content for personalized delivery. If you're already personalizing your content and need to make improvements, this step may not require much effort. However, if you've never developed personalized content before, you may require significant updates to the structure of your content and the processes you use to create it.

Some constructs you may need in your content to allow for personalization include:

- Metadata for different facets of personalization (product, user role, experience level, etc.)

- Scripts that can sort and filter your content based on the applied metadata

- A taxonomy that ensures your metadata is consistent across all content

In addition to these structural changes, your content may also require some reorganization to make personalization possible. For example, if a single deliverable contains content about multiple products, you will need to separate or label that information before you can deliver product-specific personalized content.

Once you've prepared your existing content, create a set of rules to future-proof your new content for personalization. How should content be grouped into different deliverables? What additional facets might you need over time as you personalize your content in new ways? Thinking about these questions ahead of time will help you avoid having to retrofit new content as your personalization strategy grows over time.

Support the solution

Your content may be ready for personalization, but there are several other areas where your organization will need to prepare. That's why the last step in your strategy is to make sure you have everything you need to support the solution.

The types of support you will need include:

- *Technological support.* Once your content has the right structures for personalization in place, you'll also need tools that facilitate filtering, packaging, and delivering it to your customers. Many structured content environments use a component content management system in conjunction with a dynamic delivery portal for personalization. If you're employing system-controlled personalization, you will also need a way to store and manage the data associated with each user's profile.

- *Financial support.* Adding new tools to your content workflow will cost money, so you'll need support from your managers or executives to fund your personalization strategy. You're more likely to get their buy-in if you can show them how personalization will benefit the company and estimate the return on investment.

- *Resource support.* In addition to funding, you'll need to build in time to execute your personalization strategy. You may need to invest in additional personnel to help your writers with restructuring and reorganizing your content for personalization. It's also crucial to train your content creators on any new processes related to personalization.

Content as a Service (CaaS)

Content as a Service (CaaS) means that you make information available on request. The traditional publishing model is to package and format information into print, PDF, or websites, and make those collections available to the consumer. But with CaaS, consumers decide what information they want and in what format they want it.

Giving control to the consumer

In a traditional publishing workflow, the content owner is in control until they distribute the content. After distribution, consumers take control. (A wiki is an outlier approach in which consumers can participate in content creation. From a content lifecycle perspective, a wiki expands the universe of content owners.)

Traditional publishing	CaaS
1. Write	1. Write
2. Format	2. Publish
3. Publish	3. Get content
4. Distribute	4. Format
5. Consume	5. Consume

In a CaaS environment, you transfer content ownership earlier in the process. The content owner writes and releases content, but the released content is not packaged or formatted. Instead, the raw content is made available to the consumers. Consumers can then decide which content they want, how to format it, and finally consume it.

Traditional publishing	CaaS
1. Write — *Owner* 2. Format 3. Publish 4. Distribute 5. Consume — *Consumer*	1. Write — *Owner* 2. Publish 3. Get content — *Consumer* 4. Format 5. Consume

If, as a content owner, CaaS makes you uncomfortable, it's probably because of this shift. In the content world, we are accustomed to having control over content until the last possible moment.

With CaaS, you turn over decisions about filtering, delivery, and formatting to others—a content-on-demand model. The content owner is no longer the publisher. Instead, the content consumer controls delivery; the content owner's responsibility ends when the content is made available to content consumers.

The content consumer might be a machine

In a CaaS environment, the content consumer is not necessarily a person. A CaaS environment could also supply content to a machine.

content creation   **repository**   **requestor**

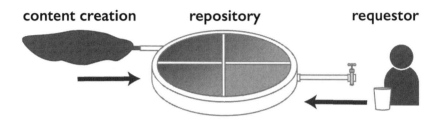

Your content consumer is likely to be software—another system in your content supply chain.

Troubleshooting Information

For example, consider a machine that you control via an on-device screen. An error occurs on the machine:

```
Error: 2785 battery low
```

Correcting the error requires troubleshooting. In the past, the troubleshooting content was loaded directly onto the machine, or perhaps a service technician might carry a tablet with troubleshooting instructions. Most machines have limited storage, so it may not be possible to load all content on them, especially if content is needed in multiple languages.

In a CaaS approach, a repository stores the troubleshooting content. When the error occurs, the machine sends the error code to the content repository along with the current language/locale setting, and the repository returns specific troubleshooting instructions.

repository   **troubleshooting**

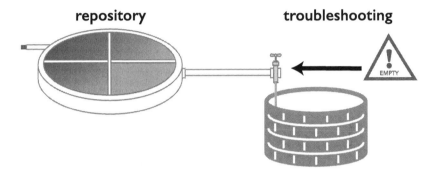

The obvious disadvantage to this approach is that it only works when your machine is connected to the content repository.

The advantages are:

- Less storage required on-device.

- Content is stored and updated centrally. No need to "push" information onto every device when there is an update.

- You can deliver troubleshooting information for that exact error code, in the appropriate language, when the machine requests it.

CaaS and chatbots

CaaS is also potentially useful for chatbots. Consider a chatbot that provides step-by-step instructions for a procedure. Instead of loading up the chatbot with huge amounts of content, you connect the chatbot to your CaaS content repository, so it delivers the procedural steps one at a time as the user goes through the procedure. Again, this approach lets you separate the chatbot's logic and processing from the text.

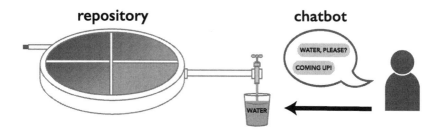

CaaS for content integration

The proliferation of multiple incompatible content repositories is a huge problem in many large organizations. There's a content management system for technical content, a learning content management system for learning/training content, a knowledge base for technical support, and so on.

The primary end user experience is generally controlled by a web CMS, and the other organizations find themselves trying to duplicate the appearance and behavior of the main website for subsites like docs.example.com or kb.example.com.

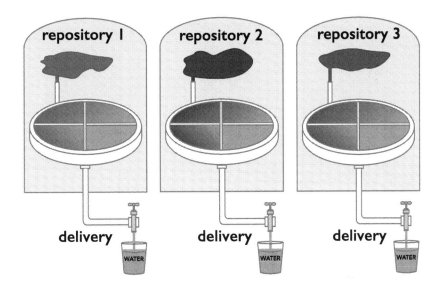

In a CaaS environment, you solve the content integration problem by making all content available to the delivery layer through content APIs. Authors create content in the various specialized systems, but delivery is managed by a single system.

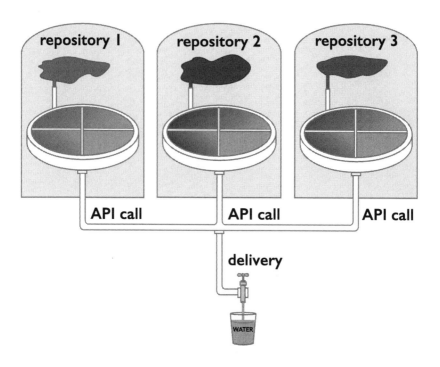

One important caveat: This approach requires systems that can communicate via APIs.

Content integration via CaaS provides a way to build out enterprise content strategy[12] without forcing every author into the same authoring system.

Component-based system architecture for CaaS

In addition to providing for content integration, a CaaS strategy could decouple the components of the

---

[12] https://www.scriptorium.com/2020/07/enterprise-content-strategy-maturity-model/

content lifecycle from the content management system. Many CMSs offer authoring and publishing, along with editing, terminology, metadata, workflows, review, and personalization[13].

You might consider a CaaS approach to separate out some of those pieces. For example, you could:

- Build sophisticated visualizations of content status for authors
- Connect with an enterprise metadata system to manage taxonomy
- Connect with an enterprise terminology system to manage metadata
- Connect the rendering system with a personalization engine

There are endless possibilities when you think about each component in the content lifecycle independently.

Getting started with CaaS

The CaaS approach opens up some fascinating possibilities and offers enormous flexibility, but it's going to be pricey to configure. You have to set up a CaaS repository and then the content consumer needs to set up CaaS requestor systems. Contrast this with traditional publishing tools or frameworks (like DITA).

---

[13] https://www.scriptorium.com/2022/01/personalized-content-steps-to-success/

If the features inside a traditional publishing tool meet your requirements, then licensing that tool is going to be the least expensive alternative. You can move up to frameworks if you need more flexibility, and up again to CaaS for maximum power, but each of these steps increases the configuration effort required.

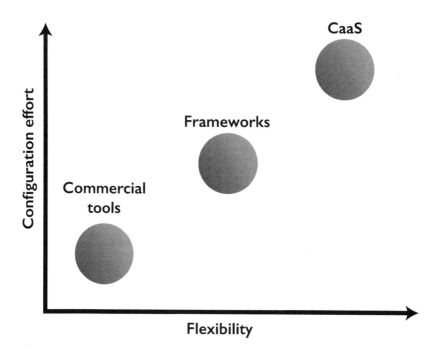

Take a look at the fundamentals of your content. To make content snippets available through a repository, you need granular, reusable content with consistent markup. Structured content offers one way to meet those requirements.

Made in the USA
Columbia, SC
14 September 2022

66916583R00054